Parentcraft

A comedy

Stephen Smith

Samuel French—London
New York-Toronto-Hollywood

ISBN 0 573 12214 8

Please see page iv for further copyright information

PARENTCRAFT

First performed at the Sawston Drama Festival on 8th
March 1996 with the following cast:

Sharon	Bernardine Orrock
Susan	Andrea Durose
Derek	Chris Shinn
Siobhan	Sally Hawley
Lesley	Jane Foskett

Produced and directed by Stephen Smith
Stage managed by Julie Petrucci
With the assistance of Martin Andrus, Edie Curtis and
Mark Easterfield

CHARACTERS

Sharon: *middle-aged*
Susan: *30s*
Derek: *30s*
Siobhan: *early 20s*
Lesley: *late 20s*

The action of the play takes place in the Parentcraft room of a maternity hospital

Time — the present

To my daughter, Kattreya,
whose birth was the inspiration for this play

Stephen Smith

Other plays by Stephen Smith published by
Samuel French Ltd

Departure
One-Sided Triangle

PARENTCRAFT

The Parentcraft room of a maternity hospital. Late autumn. Evening

A table is C of the back wall with leaflets on it; R are three stacks of chairs. There are various posters on the back wall. Positioned DR is a table with a cassette player, a carousel of cassette tapes, a large felt-tip pen and self-adhesive labels. Draped on the edge of the table is Sharon's large fake fur coat. C is a solitary chair facing R. All entrances and exits are L

When the CURTAIN *rises, music is playing from the cassette player. Sharon, a well-built middle-aged woman, has her back to the audience and is doing various exercises. After a few seconds she turns R to hold the chair for further exercises and we see in profile that she is heavily pregnant*

Susan and Derek enter. They are in their early thirties and conservatively dressed. Susan carries a bag containing her knitting

Susan (*to Sharon, sheepishly*) Excuse me.

Sharon cannot hear because of the music. Derek encourages Susan to go up to Sharon

   (*Touching Sharon on the back mid-exercise*) Excuse me.

Sharon turns round with a start and rushes to switch off the cassette player

Sharon Sorry. (*She picks up her chair and positions it alongside the table* DR)

Susan Are we the first?

Sharon We all wouldn't be here, if you were.

Susan Pardon?

Sharon The first pregnant woman. (*She takes three chairs from the stack and places them in a line for the meeting during the following*)

Susan No, I meant for the Parentcraft class.

Sharon I know what you meant, love, just pulling your leg.

Susan Oh.

Derek (*helpfully*) I get it. It's part of pain relief, isn't it?

Susan Pulling someone's leg?

Derek Humour, Susan, humour is the pain relief. Am I right?

Sharon You're right …

Derek Told you.

Sharon (*placing the third chair in front of Derek*) If you're a sadistic old sod who takes great delight in seeing his wife in pain.

Derek (*taken aback*) Do I take it you're not the instructor?

Sharon directs Susan to her seat

Sharon It's not a driving test, love. Not a question of pass or fail, more a question of not passing out. (*She returns to the cassette player*) Fancy joining me in some pelvic tilts?

Derek (*moving his chair closer to Susan and sitting down*) No, I think I'll just sit here, thank you.

Sharon (*putting her coat on the back of her chair*) I was talking to your wife. Fat lot of good it'd do you unless you're having the baby for her. Assuming she is your wife.

Derek (*shocked*) Of course she is my wife!

Sharon Don't look shocked, I bet some of the lot coming tonight won't be married.

Derek (*moving even closer to Susan*) Well we are.

Sharon Glad to hear it.

Susan Have we missed a class?

Sharon Why?

Susan Well I haven't heard anything about these pelvic tilts.

Sharon No you won't have, but the more you have the more vital they become or else everything will be around your ankles.

Derek More children you mean?

Sharon I think that's what they are called.

Susan This isn't your first then?

Sharon Eighth.

Derek Eighth! You've already had seven children!

Sharon Exactly.

Susan So what are you doing here?

Sharon (*sitting down*) Getting away from them. Great thing about being pregnant, gets you out of the house. Classes, clinics, tests: you name it — I do it. I know more about it than most of them. It's amazing how many midwives have never had a baby, you know. I mean: would you trust a chef who doesn't taste his own food?

Derek (*taking off his coat and hanging it on the back of his chair*) You don't have to be ill to be a doctor.

During the following, Derek helps Susan with her coat and then has a look at the posters

Sharon That's why they always say "This isn't going to hurt".

Susan Doesn't your husband ask why you need to keep coming to Parentcraft when you have had so many children?

Sharon Of course he does, the lazy sod, but I've told him I have to remain *au fait* with the latest medical developments. As he doesn't know what that means, he can't argue with it can he?

Susan I suppose not.

Derek (*returning to his seat*) But don't you feel it's a little irresponsible having so many children?

Sharon We all have our role in life. Mine is as a breeder. Since a teenager I discovered that getting pregnant is what I'm best at. With a falling birth rate and ageing population, people like me are going to become more valuable members of society.

Susan (*getting her knitting out of her bag*) You can't go on having children indefinitely.

Sharon No, I might declare at ten. (*She gets up*) Now, name badges.

Susan What?

Sharon We have to wear labels with our names on so that the midwife can identify us. Otherwise we'll all answer to "You with the lump under your jumper". (*She goes to the table and picks up the pen*) Now, names please.

Susan (*starting knitting for her child*) Susan and Derek.

Sharon (*writing the names on the self-adhesive labels with a large felt-tip pen*) I'm Sharon by the way. Unfortunately my writing is big and my spelling atrocious so I'll have to abbreviate. (*She sticks labels on Susan and Derek*) There we are, Suz and Del.

Derek I don't care for being called Del.

Sharon No, suits you. You should have it on your car windscreen, make you feel young again.

Derek We're not old.

Sharon Not too old to perform obviously, Del. (*She elbows him in the shoulder. Moving to Susan*) Anyway, the midwife is not going to do a lot of talking to you, is she? Personally I don't hold with all this "Husband, mop my brow" namby-pamby stuff. Get stuck in, swear like a trooper, get the bugger out, that's my motto. Call me old-fashioned but my old man hasn't seen any of ours born, if he saw what they looked like when they came out I'm sure he'd try and shove them back. (*She puts the pen and labels back on the table*)

Susan Personally I think it is very important that …

Siobhan enters. She is in her early twenties, with dyed blonde hair and very bright clothes. Although she is very well meaning she is also very stupid. She carries a shopping bag full of various jars

Sharon (*greeting Siobhan and directing her to the chair between herself and Susan*) Ah, another recruit.

Siobhan Hallo.

Sharon Park your pins over here, love. I'm Sharon, this is Suz and Del.

Derek Derek.

Sharon Oh I haven't put on my own name badge, have I?(*She goes to the table and writes "Shar" on her label*)

Susan First time?

Siobhan (*taking her coat off and sitting*) Yes.

Susan Good.

Siobhan First time for you?

Susan Yes. When is it due?

Siobhan I'm sorry, I've no idea.

Susan What?

Siobhan (*looking at Susan's baby*) I'm bad at guessing people's ages too.

Susan No, I meant *your* baby.

Siobhan Oh, sorry. In a couple of months.

Susan Could be Christmas Day then.

Siobhan Yes.

Sharon And you are?

Siobhan Twenty-three next birthday.

Sharon No, I meant your name, love.

Siobhan Siobhan.

Sharon looks horror-struck at the thought of trying to spell this

Siobhan Wilkinson.

Sharon You haven't got a second name, have you?

Siobhan No.

Sharon Ah, oh, well you'll have to be "Chev". (*She writes "Chev" on another label*)

Susan Bad luck being born near Christmas; you know everyone is going to combine the presents.

Siobhan Yes, I suppose I should have thought about that at the time. But you don't think about Christmas in March, do you?

Susan No.

Sharon (*sticking on Sioban's label*) And another customer.

Lesley enters. She is in her late twenties, well-dressed, looking like a high-flying business executive. She carries a briefcase

Lesley Good-evening.

Sharon gives Lesley a chair from the stack and directs her to sit far left next to Derek

Sharon Welcome. Your name is?

Lesley Lesley. (*She takes her seat and sits as directed*)

Sharon Oh really. You know, my gynaecologist says never trust a woman with a man's name, but I think we can make an exception for you. I'll just get your badge. Everyone else is clearly labelled. (*During the following she writes a badge for Lesley and gives it to her*)

Derek I'm Derek by the way, not Del.

Susan Susan.

Siobhan Siobhan.

Sharon So you'll be Les. At least it evens the sexes out a bit. (*She laughs*)

Lesley (*annoyed*) Are you a midwife?

Sharon No.

Lesley Then why are you taking this class?

Sharon (*sitting*) I'm not. I'm just doing my bit until the midwife comes. Bit of a flap upstairs, someone's given birth to a seagull.

Siobhan Really?

Sharon No, it's a joke. Or in Del's case, pain relief.

Siobhan Oh.

Lesley Can we take anything you say seriously?

Sharon That's up to you.

Susan (*after a pause*) You do hear some stories, though, don't you? About weird creatures being born.

Sharon You should see my family

Lesley There is no need to worry. They would spot anything on the ultrasound long before the birth.

Siobhan takes a jar of pickled onions out of her bag and starts eating them and offering them to every one else during the ensuing dialogue. They all politely decline

Sharon Or failing that they take a good look at the father.

Susan No, I'm not worried. I was just saying you hear some strange stories.

Lesley Old wives' tales most likely.

Siobhan Chinese whispers.

Lesley What?

Siobhan When something changes as it's passed along. It's called Chinese whispers.

They all look at Siobhan but she carries on munching pickled onions, oblivious

Susan (*after a pause*) Amazing, though, isn't it? Creating a new life.

Sharon Yes, I suppose it is.

Susan Every one different, having characteristics from its parents and grandparents …

Sharon And milkman.

Derek (*annoyed*) Can't you be serious?

Sharon Sorry. When you get to my level you lose all that Bambi stuff.

Lesley Actually I think having you here is destroying all the magic associated with having one's first child.

Sharon Magic! What are you going to do, pull yours out of a hat? Or have you got it stuffed up your sleeve?

Lesley Just the sort of remark I expected. I'm going to find out why the midwife hasn't turned up.

Lesley tears off her label and exits

Sharon Stuck up old cow. I'm surprised she's not got her secretary to have the baby for her.

Siobhan It is a miracle, isn't it? What you were saying about creating a new life.

Susan Yes.

Siobhan Having its own name and National Insurance number. It's made me feel quite religious.

Derek What religion are you?

Siobhan I'm not really sure. I've never really thought about it before.

Susan What are your parents?

Siobhan Man and a woman like everyone else.

Susan No, what is their religion?

Siobhan Well I never knew my father and my mother never went to church.

Derek What do you believe in?

Siobhan I'm not really sure.

Derek What about reincarnation?

Siobhan Instead of powdered milk?

Sharon You're flogging a dead horse here.

Derek Being born again. Coming back as someone else.

Siobhan Do people do that?

Derek Some think so.

Siobhan Really.

Derek Yes, if you are good in this life you'll have a better life next time round.

Siobhan What if you're bad?

Sharon You come back as Rolf Harris.

Susan What about your husband?

Siobhan (*putting the pickled onions back in her bag, embarrassed*) I'm not married.

Susan Oh dear, so you'll be a one-parent family then.

Sharon (*mouthing*) Told you so

Derek gives a disapproving look

Siobhan More like a four-parent family actually. You see I was just splitting up with Phil — he works for Securicor, looks great in a crash helmet, a bit like Robocop. Anyway, I had a brief fling with his brother Mick, he's an ice-cream man — I've got this thing about white — and met their next-door neighbour Irving — he's a male nurse — all around the same time the doctor reckons I conceived.

Sharon So it's perm any one from three.

Susan Do they know?

Siobhan Yes. They are all prepared to come to two Parentcraft classes each. It is seven classes, isn't it?

Derek I think it's eight.

Siobhan Oh dear.

Sharon You'll have to have a penalty shootout.

Susan What happens when it's born?

Siobhan I thought we'd all look at it and decide who it looks like the most.

Derek What if it only looks like you?

Siobhan Then at least I'll know it's mine.

Lesley enters

Lesley Apparently there has been a flu epidemic amongst the nursing staff and the midwife who was due to take this class is helping out upstairs. She says we can either go home or wait for

about twenty minutes when she should be free to come and have
a talk to us.

Susan We might as well wait now we're here.

Sharon We could all try some pelvic tilts.

Susan No, I think they look a bit too strenuous for me.

Siobhan Yes, better watch them do it properly at the Olympics.

Susan Sharon needs to do these exercises because she's already had
seven children.

Siobhan My God! How many are you having this time?

Sharon I didn't have them all at once.

Siobhan Sorry I thought you were one of those women that had this
fertilizer treatment.

*During the following, Lesley sits, gets a filofax from her briefcase,
puts on her glasses and starts to write busily*

Lesley So we are all going to wait are we?

Derek As long as it's not too late. I've an early start in the morning.

Susan Derek's a rep.

Sharon What's that short for: reptile?

Derek Sales Representative. I have an important meeting with a
client in Doncaster at 9.30. No doubt I'll be pounding the tarmac
while you lot are all safely tucked up in bed tomorrow morning.

Sharon Why, are you running there?

Derek No, I'll be driving in my company car.

Susan His Lada.

Derek Top of the range Lada.

Susan He has to park it around the corner, so nobody can see what
he is driving.

Derek We have all had to make sacrifices to survive the recession.

Susan He wouldn't even park in the hospital car park, we are parked
nearly half a mile away.

Derek I thought the car park would be full.

Susan At night.

Derek Yes, well, in future I will use the car park. It's all part of the
learning curve. In my job it always pays to have an open mind.

Lesley What do you sell, Del?

Derek Derek.

Lesley Derek.

Susan Castors.

Lesley Castors, oh … interesting.

Siobhan (*tucking into a jar of beetroot*) Oil or sugar?

Derek What?

Siobhan Caster oil or sugar?

Derek Wheels and associated products.

Siobhan Oh.

Derek (*getting up, full of his own importance, and parading around the room*) Yes, I sell the whole range from double ball bearing swivel castors to high quality polished brass round socket slippers.

Susan There is nothing Derek doesn't know about castors.

Derek Well, I have to admit that I do take pride in a knowledge of the widest possible selection of castors, wheels and associated products held in Europe. In fact I have been known to source many a non-standard item.

Sharon Bet you wished you hadn't asked now.

Lesley No, I find all aspects of British industry fascinating.

Derek We like to boast we are the industry that makes the wheels go round. (*He laughs*) And although Susan is right that I do have a company Lada, a slight source of irritation I must admit ——

Susan Slight!

Derek All right, a major source of irritation when all the other reps have Mondeos, but I do make it up in several different and imaginative ways. (*He stands between Sharon and Siobhan; conspiratorially*) Susan forgets our holidays in Benidorm and Sorrento which were not funded from my wage packet, I can tell you. (*He taps his nose*)

Susan Derek has a sideline making trays into skateboards and selling them to the local kids.

Lesley Really.

Derek (*moving to the cassette carousel, picking up several cassettes and looking at them*) Yes, it can be surprisingly lucrative. We even contemplated having our baby private.

Siobhan Is Del not the father?

Susan Of course Derek is the father!

Siobhan So why does he want to keep it private?

Derek (*exasperated*) I was talking about Susan using a private hospital.

Siobhan Oh. Sorry.

Susan What do you do, Lesley?

Lesley (*after a pause; looking at Derek*) I work for the Inland Revenue.

Derek Shit! (*He throws the cassettes up in the air, then scrambles to pick them up. He races up to Lesley, trying to regain his composure*) Could I get you a cup of tea, Lesley? I noticed some kitchen facilities next door.

Lesley That's very kind of you, Derek. I was told we could help ourselves. I think I'll have a black coffee if you don't mind.

Derek No, no trouble at all. Of course I'll make a contribution, we must all do our bit to help the NHS.

Lesley Most people do that by paying their taxes.

Derek Yes.

Derek exits sheepishly

Sharon Inland Revenue — hey, nice one.

Lesley It's true.

Sharon No, I believe you. It explains a lot.

Susan In Derek's defence I have to say he does like to blow his own trumpet when he hasn't really had any music lessons.

Lesley I can understand that.

Susan He likes to give the impression he is more important than he is, if you get my drift.

Sharon A snowplough would have difficulty missing that drift.

Lesley I know what you are saying.

Susan Good.

Siobhan Is Bambi a boy or a girl?

Susan Why?

Siobhan Didn't Shar say one of her children was called Bambi?

Sharon No, I didn't.

Siobhan I just thought it was a nice name. I haven't really thought about names yet.

Lesley Bambi is — or — was a boy. He is a Walt Disney animated deer.

Siobhan Bit of a girly name for a boy.

Sharon You can't knock him, did very well asking those questions on *University Challenge.*

Derek enters

Derek The kettle's on; anyone else want tea?

Siobhan That would be nice, thank you, Derek. I'll have white tea, no sugar.

Sharon Coffee for me please, Del. White with three sugars, preferably not caster.

Derek Susan?

Susan He has to ask, because he's never made it before.

Lesley All part of Parentcraft, isn't it, man training?

Susan I suppose it is. I'll have tea too, dear, no sugar.

Derek Right.

Derek exits

Sharon Are you married, Lesley?

Lesley Yes.

Sharon Haven't trained him that well then, have you?

Lesley How do you mean?

Sharon Well, where is he?

Lesley Working.

Sharon At this time of night.

Lesley He's a policeman.

Sharon So your kid's destined to be a traffic warden or a VAT Inspector.

Lesley My child will be whatever it wants to be.

Sharon I expect it will.

Siobhan I went out with a traffic warden once. You see I've got this thing about uniforms. He was a laugh. We used to play this game with these highway code signs. He had these huge display ones and we had to place them in different parts of the house. Like steep hill on the stairs, sharp bend on the landing …

Sharon Beware cattle crossing outside the bedroom?

Siobhan No, I don't think we had that one. We did have beware of the humps in the bedroom though. He was saucy for a traffic warden.

Susan What happened to him?

Siobhan He got towed away. Parked on a double yellow line in the snow. It thawed while he was at the opticians. Very sad. He couldn't live down the shame and asked for a transfer.

Susan Is your husband going to be able to attend any Parentcraft classes, Lesley?

Lesley He'll be here next week. He's on days.

Siobhan I'll have one of mine here too which will be nice.

Lesley So it'll only be Sharon without her husband then.

Sharon So.

Lesley Nothing. You raised the subject of man control.

Sharon Yes, well, the difference is I come here to get away from my husband. He's under my feet all day, not out chasing robbers like yours.

Lesley If you've already had seven children, why do you still need to come here?

Sharon Costing the taxpayer too much, is it?

Lesley No. It's just I can't see the need that's all. I can't see what you can gain from it.

Siobhan Companionship, isn't it, I understand. Getting out from behind those four walls. With all these screaming kids getting under your feet. It must be so difficult keeping an eye on seven children: that's five more than she has eyes, have you thought of that?

Sharon I can fight my own battles, thank you.

Siobhan But you shouldn't need to. You should have the chance to meet life's rich tapestry the same as the rest of us. You see, we all have other lives outside our four walls. I do my bar work, Lesley's got her tax dodgers, no offence Susan, and I expect you have a job too, Susan.

Susan I did work part-time at a newsagent's but now I'm so pregnant they thought it would put people off.

Lesley Put people off what?

Susan Buying things, I suppose.

Lesley Typical male thinking.

Susan Actually it's a woman. Indian woman. Apparently in India
  pregnant women don't work in newsagent's.

Lesley Do they have newsagents in India?

Siobhan They have cinemas. I went out with an Indian boyfriend
  once. He worked for the Post Office, I was going through a navy
  and red period. We used to go to the cinema a lot to see these Bindi
  Bhaji films. Lots of singing and jumping about, if I remember
  correctly.

Susan Anyway pregnant women are supposed to bring bad luck.
  We have to have respect for other cultures. Mrs Patel is very
  superstitious.

Siobhan I can understand that. I had this Greek boyfriend. He was
  a pilot, lovely hat. He was very superstitious; wouldn't fly his
  plane if there was bad weather.

Lesley That's not superstitious, it's being careful.

Siobhan Isn't it the same thing?

Sharon Put it this way, being superstitious doesn't prevent you
  from ending up here, being careful does.

Susan You don't want your baby, do you?

Sharon What makes you say that?

Susan Your whole attitude to pregnancy.

Sharon Do you know that some people, no matter how much
  money they have or how far medical techniques improve, will
  never be able to have children while for others it's like shelling
  peas?

Lesley If you're feeling guilty, why not put yours up for adoption?
  I'm sure there's a great shortage.

Sharon Guilty? Why should I feel guilty?

Lesley Because you are one of the fortunate shelling peas brigade.

Sharon I'm not the one who should be feeling guilty.

Lesley Well, don't look at me, this is my first. It seems to me you've
  obviously got a chip on your shoulder for some reason. As I'm not
  a psychiatrist I haven't the foggiest idea what it is.

Sharon No, you wouldn't.

Siobhan They make big ones in Belgium.

Lesley What?

Siobhan Chips. It always reminds me of a school daytrip to Ostend. The land of the big chips. That is my main memory of Belgium. Well, my only memory of Belgium actually, except for this sailor on the ferry. Lovely crisp white uniform, I expect he was an officer ... But, as that was out at sea, I don't suppose it really counts as Belgium.

Susan I went to Belgium once.

Sharon Did you?

Susan With the school hockey team. It wasn't that I was any good, it was just that my parents were one of the few families that could afford to pay for the trip. Left all our best players at home because they came from the poorer families. Even then I still didn't get into the team. I ended up as a reserve who never came on. Sums up my life, I suppose. I hope my child isn't a reserve, I want it to have a chance to play in the game.

Lesley It's dangerous to live your life again through your child.

Susan But it doesn't stop you trying to give it a better life.

Sharon You don't seem to have had a deprived childhood.

Susan No it wasn't deprived, it was very ordinary. I met Derek when I was at school. Married at eighteen. Had all these dreams, all unfullfilled. I suppose we hope that a child will change all that, bring some new meaning into our lives.

Siobhan You know, I remember them for being big, but I can't remember if it was that they were very thick or very long. The chips, I mean.

Susan French fries originated in Belgium, so I expect they were long and thin.

Siobhan That must have been it. It's Chinese chips that are very thick.

Lesley Why, have you been to China as well, then?

Siobhan No. Have you?

Lesley No.

Siobhan Well we are not that different after all then, are we. (*Pause*) Why are they called french fries if they come from Belgium?

Sharon Because they were too ashamed and wanted to embarrass the French?

Susan Or wanted to remain anonymous?

Lesley (*slamming shut her filofax and putting it into her briefcase*) This is ridiculous, I haven't come here to talk about the origins of chips.

Sharon (*sharply*) Then go.

Susan Derek will be here with your tea soon.

Lesley If the midwife doesn't turn up shortly I'm sorry but I'm going to have to go.

Siobhan The French get the blame for a lot of things don't they, like french kisses and french letters.

Susan French knickers and french leave.

Sharon French horns and french windows.

Siobhan Perhaps it was the Belgians all the time.

Susan, Sharon and Siobhan giggle like three schoolgirls

Sharon You've got a point there, Chev: on the surface the most boring country in Europe but secretly spreading their french dressing and french polish everywhere.

Susan, Sharon and Siobhan laugh together

Lesley (*obviously feeling very left out; deliberately changing the subject*) So you used to work in a newsagent's, then, Susan?

Susan Yes, only in the mornings.

Sharon Pay tax?

Susan My earnings were below the threshold.

Sharon Just protecting your interests, Suz, your husband has already dropped you in it — don't want to go down for a second time.

Siobhan Have I got a threshold?

Sharon Be careful how you answer that.

Lesley Look, I think it best we all forget I work for the Inland Revenue and avoid all conversation on barwork, newsagents, skateboards and income of any kind. I am here as a pregnant woman to learn about Parentcraft and nothing else. I'm on maternity leave anyhow.

Susan Oh good.

Sharon Stroke of luck for all concerned I'd say.

Derek enters carrying a tray of plastic cups and a plate of biscuits

Derek Tea's up.
Lesley Good.
Derek And biscuits. I put a pound in the box. Do you think that is enough, Lesley?

Derek gives Lesley a cup of tea then gives each of the others her drink and puts the tray on the table with the biscuits. Meanwhile Siobhan opens a jar of large gherkins and dunks one in her tea during the ensuing dialogue

Susan Why are you asking her?
Derek I thought she'd know about these things.
Susan She doesn't work in a hospital, you know.
Derek I know. I just thought it was more her line of country that's all.
Susan Shut up, Derek, for God's sake.
Derek Yes. Right. Well, (*he sits*) doesn't look like anyone is going to show, does it?
Lesley No.
Derek Shouldn't we all be laying down and making panting noises?
Sharon Whatever turns you on, Del.
Derek I mean this relaxation stuff; improve the circulation to your baby, reduce stress and anxiety, assist sleeping and be useful during labour.
Susan Derek did all the reading.
Derek Waiting for my number 23 at *Little Chefs* mainly. Applying my professional skills to a different area of my life. Bit of research, mind investment into a new product. Keep one step ahead of the competition.
Sharon Going into manufacturing babies then, are we?
Derek I don't think I could compete with you, Sharon. No, I'm aiming for a niche market. (*He laughs*)
Siobhan That's good, then more women will be able to work. I'm all for these niches.

Sharon If you've read so much, why don't you take the class, Del?
Susan No, I don't think that would be a very good idea.
Sharon Go on. I'm sure Derek's an expert on everything from bonk to birth.

Derek chokes on his tea

Susan (*quietly*) Derek, where is the loo? I need to go again. It's this damn tea.
Derek It's nothing to get worried about, dear. I've told you it's because your kidneys have to filter and clean fifty per cent more blood, that's all.
Susan (*putting her cup on the floor*) Derek, where is the loo?
Derek Therefore your renal function becomes more efficient with the body getting rid of waste products faster than before. You see, it's all perfectly normal.
Susan (*standing up and shouting*) Derek, where is the bloody loo!
Derek (*embarrassed*) Just down the corridor on the left

Susan exits

Siobhan You know, I think Sharon is right; why not have a go, Derek?
Derek Well, I do know this thing you do with your face.
Lesley Pardon!
Derek A relaxation method with your face. I've been practising it in traffic jams. (*Excited*) We can all try it. Can I take that for you, Lesley?

Derek leaps from his chair, takes Lesley's cup from her hand and places it on the tray. As Derek returns to the tray Siobhan offers her cup, which he duly puts on the tray, and then Sharon does the same. Derek then returns to his chair. During the following Sharon attempts to grab a biscuit

Right. Now then. First, everyone close your eyes. Come on, Sharon, close your eyes. Now just sit still and enjoy the darkness.

They all lay back in their chairs and close their eyes. There is a long pause

Siobhan (*after a long pause*) Del.
Derek Derek!
Siobhan Derek.
Derek Yes.
Siobhan I'm scared of the dark.
Derek There's nothing to be scared of, just relax. Now drag your jaw downwards.
Sharon What?
Derek Like this.
Siobhan Can we open our eyes to look?
Derek Briefly. Now feel your separated teeth.
Sharon Mine are false. I lost them with my first child.
Derek Lack of calcium, I expect.
Sharon No, he pushed me down the stairs.
Derek You'll just have to use your imagination. Relaxation is all in the mind anyway. Now you should have a heavy jaw and loose lips. Check that your tongue is in the middle of your mouth.
Siobhan (*unintelligible, with her mouth wide open*) Do we have to stick it out?
Derek What?
Siobhan (*closing her mouth*) Do we have to stick it out?
Derek No. Just let it float in your mouth.
Sharon She does that already.
Derek Now your forehead. Begin above the eyebrows and think of smoothing gently up into your hair, over the top of your head and down the back of your neck. Now just feel the tension being smoothed away.

Everyone follows Derek's instructions and all end up slouched back in their chairs with their eyes closed and mouths wide open as if they have all died of some terrible poisoning. There is a long pause

Susan enters and on reaching her chair suddenly notices the others and surveys all four in disbelief before venturing to speak

Susan Is there something wrong with the tea?

Everyone springs up

Derek No, it's the Laura Mitchell relaxation exercise for your face.
Susan Who's Laura Mitchell?
Derek I don't know. The woman who invented it I suppose.
Susan (*sitting down*) She's not that woman who has that café off the A17.
Derek Of course she isn't.
Susan You always seem to spend ages coming home when you use the A17.
Sharon He probably keeps stopping to exercise his face.
Siobhan I don't see how keeping your tongue in the middle of your mouth and dropping your jaw is going to help having a baby. Doesn't it come out the other end?
Derek The idea is to relax your whole body. That was just your face. There are exercises for your arms, legs and body as well as breathing. I'll show you if you want.
Lesley No, I think it's best to leave it to the professionals or we'll all be needing castors.
Derek Just trying to be helpful.
Lesley I know you were.
Derek Oh good. Just trying to be civic minded. Doing my bit for society.
Siobhan Do you know what? I've just realized three of our names begin with "S", isn't that a coincidence?
Lesley Yes.
Siobhan And even you have an "S" in your name, isn't that amazing? Of course most people spell my name wrong. You see Sharon only got one letter right and that's the "H". Even I spell it wrong sometimes.
Susan Irish name, is it?
Siobhan I think so. My mother just shoved a pin into a names book. My child will have a name that means something.
Sharon Like Bambi.

Siobhan No I've gone off Bambi, it's too poofy for a boy. I like Kylie.

Derek For a boy?

Siobhan No silly, for a girl. After Kylie Minogue. I'd like my daughter to be as talented. Not many people can sing and act like her.

Sharon I'd agree with that.

Derek (*after a pause, as a joke*) So I suppose it's Jason for a boy, is it?

Siobhan Now there's a thought. What a good idea. That's my names settled. Do you think naming the child is part of the Parentcraft course.

Lesley I shouldn't think so.

Siobhan It should be. I can go home tonight having achieved something. It's all thanks to you, Derek, you've named my son and relaxed my face.

Derek I'm pleased I've been helpful to someone. As they say, you mustn't judge a book by its cover.

Susan You have to if it's shrink-wrapped.

Derek Susan, you're supposed to be on my side.

Sharon But is that the right side of the tax threshold we ask ourselves.

Derek What is she on about?

Susan My job.

Derek She hasn't got you back there again, has she? I can see I'm going to have to have another word with Mrs Patel.

Susan What do you mean another word?

Derek To stop you working.

Susan It was you! She told me it was an Indian tradition.

Derek Perhaps it is. It's sensible. You shouldn't be working in your condition.

Susan Being pregnant is not a disease, Derek. It was only a few hours a week. What did you say to her?

Derek I just told her that after seven months it's illegal to employ a pregnant woman.

Susan You did what?

Siobhan Is that true? I don't want to get my pub into trouble.

Derek Do you think it's a good idea for your baby, for you to be working in a pub full of smoke? It's called passive smoking.

Siobhan I don't have a lot of choice. Although it is getting more and more difficult to fit behind the bar.

Derek You should stop like Susan.

Susan Not like Susan. Tomorrow you are going to see Mrs Patel and tell her the truth. I'll decide when I'm going to stop work.

Derek She's probably got someone else now. It's a small price to pay for the health of our child.

Susan You wouldn't say that if you were the pregnant one.

Derek Of course I would.

Siobhan You see the trouble is if I stop work I don't get paid.

Derek What about maternity leave.

Siobhan I can't get that.

Derek Why?

Siobhan Close your ears, Lesley. (*Whispering*) It's all cash in hand. You know what I mean, Derek. Being in the same game yourself.

Lesley looks at Derek

Derek (*nodding in agreement until he catches Lesley's eye*) Well not exactly. In fact I would like to set the record straight on that subject. In case anyone got the wrong impression, I have made very few skateboards.

Sharon You do surprise me, Del.

Derek And the ones I have made have all been passed on, at cost, as a kind of humanitarian gesture to the less privileged.

Sharon That's not what you said earlier.

Derek No, well, I was being somewhat economical with the truth.

Sharon Or the kids, if you knocked off the castors in the first place.

Derek I didn't knock off the castors, they were seconds, they were going to be thrown out anyway.

Sharon So they are dangerous then.

Derek Of course they are not dangerous. They just have some paint missing or minor scratches. Our Quality Control Department is the finest in the European Community. The merest imperfection and they reject automatically.

Sharon So how can it be at cost if you got them for free.

Derek sits open-mouthed, frantically searching his brain for another excuse until, realizing he is beaten, he explodes with anger

Derek Look, I have come here for a Parentcraft class not an interrogation. (*He looks at his watch impatiently*) I think it's about time I found out if this midwife is going to speak to us or not.

Derek rushes off

Sharon Why didn't you say Lesley is on maternity leave?

Susan Two can play at being economical with the truth.

Siobhan Now you're not working, Susan, I expect you spent the day watching the soaps on TV.

Susan Not exactly.

Siobhan Godsend this satellite TV, it really fills my day. You can see them all again. I like the Australian ones best, they are more like us than the Americans. In fact the only difference between the Australians and us is that they have another name for Marmite.

Lesley I think there are a few other differences.

Siobhan That's the weather, it's the climate and the fact that they all live around the edge of Australia. It wouldn't be realistic to walk into the *Rovers Return* carrying a surfboard. (*Pause*) You know that's the one present Santa Claus wouldn't have to bring down the chimney.

Lesley What a surfboard?

Siobhan No, a satellite dish. Unless of course you opt for cable.

Sharon Has anyone ever told you, you've got a strange mind?

Siobhan No, why, have I?

Sharon It's either that or Derek's spiked your tea.

Siobhan It was the thought of my child being born on Christmas Day, that's all. Of course one advantage would be I could avoid explaining the facts of life. I know I'm going to find that very embarrassing. I could say Santa Claus brought it down the chimney. Of course we would have to move out of the flat and into a house first.

Susan When are you due, Sharon?

Sharon For sprog number eight? December 14th. Which will be my first December child. I've already got a November and January. I try to spread them out during the year as much as possible.

Susan What are their names?

Sharon Barney, Paddington, Parsley, Orinoco, Bungo, Rosie and Jim. Like Siobhan, I wanted my children to have meaningful names.

Susan What are you going to call yours, Lesley?

Lesley We haven't decided yet.

Susan No, neither have we. Derek wants Derek Junior for a boy but I'm not that happy. I quite like Ivor but as our surname is Coxhead, it wouldn't be a very good idea.

Siobhan (*singing*) Do your ears hang low,

> Do they wobble to and fro,
> Can you tie them in a knot,
> Can you tie them in a bow,
> Can you toss them over your shoulder,
> Like a regimental soldier,
> Do your ears hang low?

(*Speaking*) Funnily enough I learnt that from a soldier. Didn't stay with him that long, I'm not that much into green. But it'll come in handy for getting my child off to sleep so it wasn't a wasted experience.

Derek enters

Derek (*very smugly*) You'll never guess what I've just found out?

Susan The source of the M25?

Derek No, a very interesting piece of information. I was chatting to the midwives upstairs about this assembled throng and was asked to describe one of our number in detail. It transpires that we have a cuckoo in the nest, one of our potential mothers isn't even pregnant.

Siobhan Ante-natal I expect.

Derek What?

Siobhan When somebody doesn't want a child. Pre-natal if you want one and ante-natal if you don't; I have done some studying you see.

Lesley What's post-natal then?

Siobhan Er … isn't that when you have a test-tube baby? Originally the test tube was sent in the post so the donor remained anonymous.

Derek This woman is not pregnant at all, she is pretending.

Susan What are you on about Derek?

Derek Elizabeth Longhurst is her name.

Susan But there's nobody called that here.

Derek Exactly. She has come under a false name, because she has a thing about pretending to be pregnant.

Sharon A fantasy about being pregnant, a chance to try and experience what she has been denied, you mean?

Derek I suppose so, Elizabeth (*pointing to his label*) or should that be Liz?

Susan You mean it's Sharon?

Derek Apparently so.

Lesley Is this true?

Sharon (*getting up and putting on her coat and gloves and putting her chair away*) This could have been my finest hour if you hadn't turned up. I could have been wife, mum and midwife all rolled into one with the other three and they would have been none the wiser. Not everyone can adopt or have fertility treatment, you know. Some of us are just too old, too poor, or just not important enough. It soon becomes easier to pretend to be a real woman. Somebody special, even superior — find imperfections in others. It just lets a little light into a very dark room.

Lesley I really think you should see someone about this.

Sharon Don't worry, I'm not likely to abduct someone else's child. No point punishing others for the sins of nature, however much you are tempted.

Susan I'm very sorry.

Sharon It's no need for you to be sorry, it's not your fault. (*She collects her handbag*) I suppose they've called the police?

Derek I think so.

Sharon They said they would after last time. Interesting offence, impersonating a pregnant woman.

Derek (*sympathetically*) I'd go if I were you.

Sharon Quite right, Del, save embarrassment. We can't have Lesley's husband turning up to arrest me, Siobhan may make a dive for the white stripes on his uniform.

Derek I didn't mean that …

Sharon I know what you mean. You think they'll lock me up in a looney bin and throw away the key, don't you?

Derek Not exactly.

Sharon (*walking up to Derek*) Just one word of advice, Derek: lay off the face exercises or they'll be locking you up.

Sharon exits

Susan Poor woman.

Derek (*sitting*) I feel like a right bastard now.

Lesley Don't worry, Derek, we were going to find out sooner or later — it was probably better we found out sooner.

Siobhan opens a jar of Branston pickle and starts eating

Derek Apparently a student midwife took the last course and our so-called Sharon lasted four classes until a senior midwife spotted her in the corridor.

Lesley Quite a revelation, Derek, and all because she was goading you over your skateboards.

Derek Yes, about them ——

Susan She's on maternity leave, Derek, she doesn't care.

Derek Don't you?

Lesley I wouldn't say I didn't care, more it's none of my business.

Derek So I've been doing all this bowing and scraping for nothing.

Lesley I appreciated it, Derek.

Derek And you knew all the time?

Susan Sort of.

Derek Well thanks a bunch. It's the last time I try to earn some spare cash for your whims.

Lesley Derek, is this midwife coming or not?

Derek Probably not, apparently this going into labour has a somewhat flexible duration. She suggests we come back next week.

Lesley (*putting her coat on*) Good idea, I'm off. I've had enough excitement for one evening. (*She picks up her chair and puts it back on the stack*)

Derek and Susan put on their coats. Siobhan puts away her pickles

I'll see you all next week then.

Derek Right.

Susan Good-night.

Siobhan Bye.

Lesley exits

Siobhan puts on her coat

Derek (*putting Susan's chair on the stack*) What a waste of an evening that was.

Susan Better luck next week, I hope. (*She picks up her cup and places it on the table* c)

Derek collects Siobhan's chair

Siobhan (*approaching Susan with her back to Derek*) Er, Susan, did I hear you have a car?

About to put Siobhan's chair on the stack, Derek frantically tries to signal "No" to Susan

Susan Er … Yes.

Derek slams the chair down on the stack

Siobhan I wonder if I could cadge a lift.

Susan That won't be a problem will it, Derek?

Derek (*aggressively*) No.

Siobhan turns to look at Derek and he forces a smile. He walks towards Susan but Siobhan stops him

Siobhan You know who I feel most sorry for?
Derek No?
Siobhan Sharon's other seven children.

Derek and Susan look at each other

Black-out

FURNITURE AND PROPERTY LIST

On stage: Three stacks of chairs
                Table. *On it*: practical cassette player, carousel of cassette
                    tapes, large felt-tip pen, self-adhesive labels, large fake fur
                    coat for **Sharon**
                Chair

Off stage: Bag containing knitting (**Susan**)
                Bag containing jars of pickled onions, gherkins, Branston
                    pickle (**Siobhan**)
                Briefcase containing filofax, pair of spectacles (**Lesley**)
                Tray of plastic cups of tea, plate of bisuits (**Derek**)

LIGHTING PLOT

Practical fittings required: nil
Interior. The same scene throughout

To open: General interior lighting

Cue 1   **Derek** and **Susan** look at each other   (Page 28)
          Black-out

EFFECTS PLOT

No cues